SELL LIKE A KING

SELL LIKE A KING

HIMANSHU MITTAL

First Printing, 2025

CONTENTS

DEDICATION

This book is dedicated to my mother, who built a future for me when the present had nothing to give. For every silent sacrifice, every unseen tear, every hope whispered in the dark, you were my first and greatest lesson in resilience. This book exists because you never gave up.

ACKNOWLEDGMENTS

First, to my wife, Kanchan, this book exist because of you. You took the weight of our world onto your shoulders so mine could remain free to build. You managed our home, nurtured our child, and guarded my peace—all without a word of complaint, even when our means were thin. You saw my potential when all I could see was pressure, and you encouraged me to take the very risks that now define our life. Your greatest gift was your faith. You left your own noble career as a teacher, not with resignation, but with a fierce, strategic decision to bet on us. That selfless courage provided the unwavering foundation upon which every success in these pages is built. For your sacrifices, your strength, and your stunning belief in me—thank you. This is as much your victory as it is mine.

My profound gratitude to my mentor, Mr. Amol Karale. You saw the raw material and taught me how to forge a positive mindset. Your guidance was the catalyst that shifted my vision from what I lacked to what I could create. Thank you for the lessons that transcended business and shaped my life.

To my spiritual guide, S.N. Goenka, and the transformative practice of Vipassana. Your teachings provided the quiet ground upon which a noisy mind could find clarity. They taught me to observe, to understand, and ultimately, to master my own behavior. The equanimity and self-awareness I strive for are gifts of your wisdom.

To every client who took a chance on me. In my earliest days, when I had little more than a desperate hunger to prove myself, you offered trust. You believed not in my track record, but in my intent. Your faith was the currency that purchased my confidence, and your partnerships are the bedrock of the professional I am today. Thank you for your business, and for the priceless gift of your belief.

Last but not least, my sincere thanks to Mr.Hemsingh Patle, Mr. Manoj Sonawane and BLISS Books editotorial team who helped me to publish the content of this book.

And finally, to you, the reader. By choosing this book, you are choosing to build. I honour your journey and the ambition that brought you here.

Love & Gratitude
Himanshu Mittal

INTRODUCTION

STOP SELLING START BECOMING

If you picked up this book, you're probably looking for answers. Maybe you're tired of:

- Hearing "no" more often than "yes"
- Working twice as hard for half the results
- Watching competitors win deals you deserved
- Feeling that knot in your stomach before making calls
- Wondering if you're truly cut out for sales

I know these feelings intimately. I was once the salesman nobody wanted to buy from—the invisible kid from the tin shed who couldn't afford confidence.

But what if I told you that your biggest weakness is actually your greatest advantage? That the very thing you're trying to hide—your background, your struggles, your insecurities—could become your most powerful selling tool?

This isn't just another sales book. This is a transformation manual.

The 48-Hour Transformation Challenge

Most people will read this book over weeks. They'll highlight a few lines, maybe take some notes, then go back to their old habits.

But you're different.

I challenge you to read this book cover-to-cover in the next 48 hours. Why? Because real change happens fast or not at all. Your breakthrough is waiting, but it demands your complete immersion.

What You'll Discover in This Book:

Part 1: The Inner Foundation (Chapters 1-4)
You'll learn why mindset isn't fluffy motivation—it's the bedrock of every sale you'll ever make. We'll rebuild your confidence from the ground up, using lessons forged in poverty and desperation.

Part 2: The Art of Connection (Chapters 5-7)
Discover how to build unshakeable trust in minutes, not months. Learn the questioning framework that uncovers what clients truly want (even when they don't know themselves).

Part 3: Mastering the Game (Chapters 8-9)
Transform objections into opportunities and learn why premium clients actually prefer paying more. Plus, the digital strategies that let you scale your impact beyond face-to-face meetings.

The Secret Nobody Tells You About Sales

For years, I chased the "perfect pitch." I studied closing techniques, practiced handling objections, and tried to sound like someone I wasn't.

Then I discovered the truth: **People don't buy your product. They buy your belief in it.** And before they can believe in your product, they need to believe in you.

This book will show you how to:

- Turn your deepest struggles into your strongest value proposition
- Command attention without saying a word
- Create such undeniable value that price becomes irrelevant
- Build a personal brand that attracts clients to you
- Develop the unshakeable confidence of someone who knows their worth

My journey began in a house that leaked when it rained. I slept hungry more nights than I care to remember. I lost my mother too young and found myself homeless at nineteen. The voice in my head constantly whispered, "You're not good enough."

But that same voice became my greatest teacher. Those same struggles became my competitive advantage.

Now, I'm going to show you how to transform your liabilities into assets, your fears into fuel, and your past into your most compelling sales pitch.

The only question is: Are you ready to stop selling and start becoming?

Your transformation begins the moment you turn this page. The 48-hour clock starts now.

CHAPTER 1

I am the Loser in My Story

"It is not the lion's size, but his hunger, that makes him king." — ***African Proverb***

I was born in a small town, into a humble family. My father was a salesman, and my mother was a housewife. We lived in a modest two-room house—one with a cemented roof and the other with a tin shed.

Our world was two rooms wide. One with a cemented roof for my parents, the other a tin shed where my two younger brothers and I learned life's hardest lessons. The shed taught us about heat that suffocates, cold that seeps into bones, and rain that finds every gap like destiny finding its target. When the monsoons came, we'd place utensils under the leaks, creating a symphony of *plink, plink, plink*—the sound of temporary fixes for permanent problems.

The invisible boy

At school, I was the invisible kid—the one who barely spoke, who was often made fun of, and who secretly wished to shine but never had the courage to step forward. I was an average student at best, barely passing my exams, sometimes only with grace marks. Teachers saw me as just another below-average student, and my classmates either ignored me or ridiculed me. I was short, dark, thick, and unremarkable. Friends? I had one or two at most.

My parents struggled to pay my school fees, yet they held onto the hope that I would achieve something great. But I felt the weight of their expectations pressing heavily on my naïve shoulders.

When I reached the ninth standard, I timidly asked my mother if I could take tuition classes. I dared not ask my father, fearing his anger. My mother, despite having no money, agreed without hesitation. A month later, I asked for another tuition, and then another. Soon, my tuition fees exceeded my school fees. My mother, who had never worked before, took up home-based handicraft work just to cover the costs. Looking back, I don't know if I took those classes to genuinely learn or if I simply wanted to prove to my classmates that I could afford what they could.

The household tyrant

My father was a daily drinker. His return home was a dreaded event, marked by verbal abuse and violence. My mother bore the brunt of his anger, but my brothers and I were not spared. It became so routine that we no longer reacted. He looked down upon us—his wife was not educated and modern, and his children were not fair or smart enough to be paraded in front of his relatives and friends.

I remember that once we had to go to a function all together so my father left home first and went alone and asked us to leave after some time and reach separately just to avoid drawing people's attention to our large family. He lived his life freely, traveling and socializing, but never made us a part of it.

He often told me to quit school and start working at a tea stall, calling me good-for-nothing. It was my mother who fought for my education, pleading and enduring more beatings just to keep me in school.

A mother's silent tears

One day, our world shattered. We discovered that my father was having an affair and spending all his money on another woman. My grandmother confronted him, but he responded by throwing her out of the house. I was fifteen, old enough to understand the betrayal but too afraid to challenge him. When I gathered the courage to ask him to take care of my mother, he coldly threatened, "I will kill myself if you don't mind your own business."

My mother, who had always treated my father as her god, was devastated. She endured everything silently, not wanting her children to grow up in a broken home. But her heartbreak took its toll—she was diagnosed with high blood pressure and kidney failure within a year. Our lives turned upside down.

Gone were the days of playing video games and cricket in the streets. I now spent my time cooking, cleaning, taking care of my mother, and rushing to hospitals three times a week for her dialysis. We couldn't afford private healthcare, so we relied on government hospitals, which were overcrowded and unhygienic. My mother became bedridden, unable to even go to the washroom without help. She wept in helplessness, ashamed that her son had to assist her with such intimate tasks. I wept in silence, unable to ease her pain.

My first income

I was living in a society where our neighbors were rickshaw drivers, auto mechanics, street vendors, and laborers. I respect their profession and value their hard work, but it was not helping me in any way to make money for my family. With no internet access and no real opportunities, I had limited options—work at a tea stall or as a helper in a shop.

As my mother's condition worsened, we had to sell half of our house. There were nights we had no food. I could no longer watch my family suffer. That was the moment I, Himanshu Mittal, decided to stop being a boy and become a man.

I was in 12th standard and my board exams were approaching but due to our worsening financial condition, I had to look for work. Through a reference, I got a job at an iron factory unloading trucks. I carried long iron rods and grills on my shoulders during the night shift, earning a mere ₹130 (less than $2). The next day, I sat for my board exams. After a week, the excruciating pain in my legs and back forced me to quit. But, I couldn't afford to stay at home, so I started working in sales.

I used to ride my bicycle and sell various items like perfume bottles, caps, belts, rings, and similar goods. I had no experience in sales, and my clothes were shabby, so most shopkeepers wouldn't let me enter their shops. Some even threatened to call the police, suspecting that I had stolen these items. Those who did choose to buy from me wanted the items at the cheapest rates and on credit. After a lot of rejection in the main market, I turned to small towns and villages where people at least listened to me, even if margins were lower. I kept on going.

Homeless and alone

Eventually, I found work at a computer institute as a sales representative, placing standees on roads and convincing students to enroll. Amidst this routine of struggle—waking up, cooking, cleaning my mother's bed, working, studying, and hospital visits—life dealt its hardest blow. My mother passed away, leaving behind a void that nothing could fill.

Her suffering ended, but mine did not. My father remarried within nine months, and there was no place for me in his new life. I left home (I never returned to that house again) and went to a different city to pursue my studies. At nineteen, I was alone, homeless, with nothing but a single trouser and two shirts. I had no money, no shelter, no family to turn to. To survive, I worked as a cashier at KFC, delivered couriers, and gave home tuition. Despair consumed me. I tried to end my life—twice from a rooftop, once on railway tracks. But each time, something held me back. A whisper of survival, a sliver of hope.

I had reached rock bottom. But rock bottom was also where I found my strength. This was not the end of my story—it was just the beginning.

CHAPTER 2

The Real Battle: Inner Game vs. Outer Game

"The greatest discovery of my generation is that a human being can alter his life by altering his attitudes". - ***William James***

Let me ask you something straight — have you ever felt like you're doing *everything right* in sales but still not getting the results you deserve? You're showing up, making calls, sending follow-ups, watching motivational videos, maybe even reading sales books... yet something feels off.

I've been there. And trust me, the problem isn't your product, your pitch, or your market.

The real problem sits quietly between your ears — in that small voice that keeps whispering:-

"I'm not good enough..."
"Why does this always happen to me?"
"I can't handle another rejection..."

I Was Living in My Mind

No wonder my background shaped my beliefs long before I entered sales. a two-room house, financial struggles, and a father who made me feel invisible.

I grew up thinking *people like me don't get rich, it is difficult to make money, rich people are arrogant etc.* That success was meant for those who spoke English fluently, dressed sharply, or came from "good families."

So when I entered sales, I carried that baggage with me.

Whenever I sat across a client in a fancy office, my body was there — but my confidence wasn't.

My mind would whisper, *"He's successful and rich... he won't listen to you."*

The irony was crushing. I was a salesman, just like my father. But where his failures filled him with anger, mine filled me with a deep-seated belief that I didn't belong.

This wasn't a new feeling. It was a ghost I'd carried from a childhood that taught me people like us don't get a seat at the table. I walked into every meeting already defeated, not by the client, but by the story I was telling myself.

Even before I opened my mouth, I had already lost the deal — not in reality, but in my imagination.

"Whether you think you can or think you can't — you're right." — Henry Ford

My outer world was just a reflection of my inner world.

The Power of Inner Game

You can learn all the closing techniques in the world — but if your *inner game* is broken, no tactic will save you.

Your mindset, beliefs, and self-image decide how you show up before the client does.

For the longest time, my self-talk was brutal.

"I'm not smart enough."

"I'm not good-looking."

"They won't take me seriously."

Every time someone said "no," it wasn't just a rejection of my offer — it felt like a rejection of *me.*

I kept telling myself these stories so often that they became my reality.

And life, being an obedient servant, kept giving me proof that I was right.

Then one day, my mentor said something that hit me like lightning:

"Your results are derived by your own thoughts."

That single sentence changed everything.

Reprogramming the Mind

Around that time, I picked up a book — *The Power of Your Subconscious Mind* by Dr. Joseph Murphy.

It taught me a truth I'll never forget:

Your mind is like fertile soil — it doesn't care what you plant, it just grows whatever seed you give it.

If you plant doubt, you harvest hesitation.

If you plant faith, you harvest courage.

The book became my bible. I decided to replant my mind.

Every morning, I spoke to myself differently.

I said things like, "I'm learning fast." "I add value." "People enjoy buying from me."

At first, it felt fake — but here's the twist: *so did my old doubts when I first believed them.*
Both were lies; I just chose a better one this time.

And slowly, my energy shifted. I started walking into meetings with calm confidence.
My tone changed. My body language changed.
Clients could feel that I believed in myself — and they began to believe in me too.

"Words are, of course, the most powerful drug used by mankind." — *Rudyard Kipling*

Owning Your Results

Once I stopped blaming the market, leads, or my luck — everything started to move.
The day you take 100% responsibility for your results is the day you stop being a victim and start becoming a creator.

I built three daily habits that helped me rewire my inner game:

1. **Gratitude every morning** – I started my day by thanking what I already had. Gratitude kills scarcity.
2. **Positive self-talk** – I replaced my inner critic with an inner coach.
3. **Reflection every night** – Instead of saying "Why me?", I asked "What did I learn today?"

These tiny shifts did something incredible — they made my confidence *real*.
Not loud. Not fake. Just quietly certain.

The Tale of Two Wolves

An old man sat with his grandson by the warmth of a cooking fire. The evening was quiet, but the boy could sense a restlessness in his grandfather.

"Something troubles you, Grandfather?" the boy asked.

The old man nodded slowly, his eyes reflecting the flickering flames. "There is a battle raging inside me," he confessed. "A fight between two wolves."

The boy leaned closer, intrigued.

"The first wolf," the grandfather explained, "is darkness. He is carried by the winds of anger, jealousy, and regret. His steps are heavy with greed and his voice echoes with arrogance. He feeds on self-pity and guilt, and his shadow is cast by lies and false pride."

The boy's eyes widened. "And the other wolf, Grandfather?"

"The second wolf is light," the old man said, his voice softening. "He runs with joy and peace in his heart. His path is guided by love and his strength comes from hope. He carries with him humility, kindness, and compassion. He speaks only truth and gives generously without expecting anything in return."

The boy thought for a long moment, watching the fire dance between them. "But Grandfather," he finally asked, "which wolf will win this terrible fight?"

The old man placed a gentle hand on the boy's shoulder, his eyes holding generations of wisdom. **"The one I choose to feed, my child. Always, the one I choose to feed."**

The Truth About the Inner and Outer Game

Here's what I've learned after more than a decade in sales:

Your *outer game* (your pitch, product, and presentation) only amplifies your *inner game.*

You can't out-hustle a weak belief system.
You can't fake conviction for long.
People don't buy your product — they buy your energy, certainty, and belief.

The moment you start believing, "I am valuable," you start attracting clients who see that value.

Once I changed the conversation inside my head, something surprising happened — I stopped fearing people.
I started picking up the phone with excitement instead of anxiety.
I began reaching out to clients I once thought were "out of my league."

And suddenly, meetings that felt impossible before started opening up.

That's when I learned — **prospecting isn't about getting a meeting; it's about becoming the person worth meeting.**

Key Takeaways:

- Your background is not your boundary; it's just your beginning.
- Your subconscious mind obeys your words — speak power, not doubt.
- You don't need more motivation; you need a new internal language.
- The outer game only works when the inner game is aligned.
- Believe first. Sell later.

CHAPTER 3

The Art of Securing Sales Meetings

*"You miss 100% of the shots you don't take." – **Wayne Gretzky***

When I started my sales career, I had no idea how much courage it took to pick up the phone. I'd stare at the number, rehearse what I'd say, imagine being ignored, judged, or rejected — and by the time I finally called, my energy was already drained.

If you've ever hesitated before dialing, I know exactly how you feel. That small voice in your head starts whispering:

"What if he hangs up?"
"She must be busy."
"I'll call later — maybe next week."

Here's the truth: **the call you don't make is the opportunity you'll never get.**

The Shift: From Fear to Intention

The biggest realization I ever had was this — **the goal of a sales call is not to sell. It's to secure a meeting.**

That shift alone made me fall in love with prospecting. Because now, every call wasn't a do-or-die attempt to close; it was just an invitation to a conversation.

When I believed that, my voice changed. My hesitation disappeared. I stopped "convincing" and started *connecting.*

And that's where it all begins — with your **energy**.

"People may hear your words, but they feel your attitude." *–John C. Maxwell*

Even over the phone, they can sense whether you're confident or desperate, calm or chaotic.

You may not see them, but they can *feel* you.

That's why every successful call starts before you even dial. Sit straight. Smile. Remind yourself — *I'm not disturbing; I'm delivering value.*

Your background might not be privileged (mine wasn't either — you already know that from Chapter 1), but your voice can still carry authority.

Confidence doesn't come from where you come from — it comes from what you *believe* you bring to the table.

The Power Pitch: Simplicity Wins

Let's talk about the structure of your pitch — the 30 seconds that decide whether you're trusted or forgotten.

Forget memorizing complicated scripts. You don't need that. What you need is a **skeleton** — a clear *structure* you can personalize to any product or service.

Here's the skeleton:

1. **Start with warmth and energy.**
   People can feel your smile through the phone.

"Hi [Name], this is [Your Name] from [Company]. How are you doing today?"

2. State the reason you're calling.

Be honest, clear, and direct. This is crucial and will decide if the listener will continue to be on the call or not.

"The reason I'm calling is because I recently helped a few people in your area find homes that fit their budget perfectly, and I thought of reaching out to you as well."

3. Add a relevant hook.

Link what you do to what *they might want.* Specify the outcome.

"Many people I talk to are either looking to upgrade or invest for rental income — does that sound like something you're exploring too?"

4. Ask for a short, specific meeting.

Make it easy to say yes. Be positive and excited as it is obvious to get a yes.

"I'd love to set up a quick 15-minute meeting this week to understand your needs better and see if I can help. Would Tuesday or Wednesday work better for you?"

That's it. No over-explaining. No desperation. No long monologues. **And here's how it sounds in real life (And you can use it in your industry):**

"Hi Mr. Sharma, this is Himanshu calling from Shapesky Realty. How are you doing today?

The reason I'm calling is — we recently helped a few families in your area move into new homes at great locations, and I wanted to check if you're considering any property purchase or investment this year.

PAUSE (wait for them their response)

I'd love to schedule a short 15-minute discussion to understand your goals and share what's working in today's market. Would tomorrow or Wednesday work better for you?"

That's it — short, relevant, confident.

And if you're in insurance, it's the same structure — just change the context:

"Hi Meena, this is Rahul calling from FutureLife Insurance. The reason I'm calling is we've been helping professionals like you create tax-free retirement plans.

PAUSE

I'd love to understand your goals and see if this could benefit you too.

PAUSE

Does Tuesday evening or Wednesday morning work better for a 15-minute chat?"

Don't Memorize — Internalize

Once you understand the skeleton, you'll never need to memorize anything. Because now, instead of trying to *sound* like a salesperson, you'll sound like a *human who knows what they're doing.*

Sales is like a conversation between two equals — not a teacher and a student, not a beggar and a king.

Your tone should say: "I respect your time, but my time is valuable too."

That's what makes people listen.

The Rule: Always Book a Meeting from a Meeting

Never end a conversation with, *"I will connect with you later."* That's the fastest way to lose control of your pipeline.

Top sales performers have a simple habit: before ending any call or meeting, they *book the next one.*

It could be a demo, a discussion, or even a follow-up — but it's *scheduled.*

You don't leave the ball hanging in the air; you place it in your calendar.

"Always book a meeting from a meeting."

This habit alone can multiply your sales rhythm. Because now, you don't wake up wondering, *"Whom should I call today?"* — your day is already full.

So, you go like "*Thank you for your time today! Let's connect again on Tuesday at 3 PM.*"

The Month I Had No Meetings

There was a month early in my career when I thought I was working hard.

I would reach the office on time, open my laptop, stare at my CRM, and tell myself I was "planning my day."

In reality, I was hiding behind the illusion of productivity.

I'd polish my pitch deck, tweak my proposal, check LinkedIn, and convince myself I was being strategic. But deep down, I knew the truth — I wasn't calling, I wasn't following up, and I definitely wasn't booking enough meetings.

My calendar looked like a white desert.

No meetings. No follow-ups. Just blank spaces that made me feel busy but broke.

By the end of that month, I had no new leads and no energy. I was frustrated, blaming the market, the product, even my luck. That's when I learned from Grant Cardone's coaching program that changed everything:

"An empty calendar is not peace — it's a warning."

That line hit me like a punch in the gut. Because it was true. I had confused peace with passivity. Comfort with control.

The next month, I decided to fill my calendar like my life depended on it.

I made calls until my throat went dry. I booked follow-ups even if the prospect didn't sound promising. I double-scheduled meetings and ran from one location to another like a madman.

It wasn't perfect — some meetings got canceled, others led nowhere.

But something shifted inside me.

When your calendar is full, your mind stays sharp.

You don't chase clients out of desperation; you choose who deserves your time.

You don't wait for opportunities; you *create* them.

By the end of that month, my confidence had doubled. I wasn't afraid of rejection anymore — because even if one deal didn't close, I had five more lined up.

Since that day, I made a rule for myself: **No white space in the calendar. Ever.**

Because in sales, a white calendar is like an empty chair in a restaurant — it doesn't matter how good your food is if no one's sitting down to taste it.

That experience taught me something I now call *The White Space Principle* — if your calendar isn't full, your pipeline never will be.

The Story of the Dabbawala who Became a Sales Manager

A young man from a traditional family in Pune, Rohan, got his first sales job. For the first month, he did what everyone did: he waited for leads from marketing, sent a few emails, and made a handful of calls. His calendar was a desert of white space.

Frustrated, he thought of his uncle, a Mumbai Dabbawala. He realized their entire system was built on a principle: **no tiffin is ever left undelivered.** Every slot in their delivery cycle is accounted for; there is no "white space."

Rohan applied this to his calendar. He blocked out two-hour "delivery slots" every day solely for prospecting. If a meeting got canceled, that slot wasn't empty—it was immediately filled with 10 quick calls, just like a Dabbawala would immediately reroute a delivery.

He stopped waiting. He started delivering his pitch with the same relentless consistency. Within six weeks, he was the top performer. He didn't have better scripts; he had a fuller calendar. The **Dabbawala's Discipline** eliminated his white space and filled his pipeline.

The White Space Principle

White spaces on your calendar are the devil. They look peaceful but are dangerous.

They mean your momentum is dying.

Your calendar should look like a battlefield — packed with meetings, calls, follow-ups.

If you find empty slots, fill them with something productive — cold calls, prospect research, or training.

Here's a trick I learned: **double-book sometimes.**

Yes, you may have to drop one, but that's okay. It gives you **choice. Choice gives you power.**

A packed calendar is not stress — it's certainty.

"Success is nothing more than a few simple disciplines, practiced every day." – Jim Rohn

Final Thought

Every meeting you secure is a door — behind one of them could be your biggest deal yet.

But that door won't open by itself. You'll have to knock.

The difference between an average salesperson and a top performer is **not talent — it's consistency.**

Top performers don't wait for the "mood." They dial anyway.

So tomorrow, when you pick up your phone, don't think about rejection or outcomes.

Just remind yourself:

"I'm not interrupting. I'm introducing possibility."

Smile. Dial. Book that meeting.

And remember — that's where your next success story begins.

Your Turn:

Tomorrow morning, before you open your inbox, list at least ten names you'll call — not to sell, but to *book meetings*. Track how many calls it takes to get one "yes." That number is your truth. Once you know it, control it.

And remember: empty calendar = empty pipeline = empty wallet. Fill it. Guard it. Build it.

CHAPTER 4

The Salesperson's Superpower: Energy & Identity

The one thing you can't take away from me is the way I choose to respond to what you do to me. The last of one's freedoms is to choose one's attitude in any given circumstance. - ***Viktor Frankl***

I remember the day I discovered my real superpower. It wasn't a perfect pitch or a clever closing technique. It was 8 AM, and I had just received news that made my stomach drop. The deal I had been counting on for months had fallen through.

An hour later, I had my most important meeting of the month.

The old me would have rescheduled. The old me would have brought that defeated energy into the room. But that morning, I made a choice. I stood outside the office building, closed my eyes, and made a decision: **For the next hour, I would be the most positive and energetic person my client had ever met.**

I didn't fake it. I transformed.

The Choice That Changes Everything

Sales is the profession of daily rejection. We face more "no's" before lunch than most people face in a month. And that's exactly why our attitude is our greatest asset.

I learned this not in a fancy training room, but on the streets, selling perfume bottles to shopkeepers who didn't want to see me. Some days, the rejections would pile up so high I wanted to quit. But I noticed something: when I approached the next shop with a genuine smile and positive energy, the conversation changed. Not always, but often enough to keep me going.

Your mood is not a reaction to your circumstances. It's a choice you make before you pick up the phone or walk through the door.

The Story of the Auto-rickshaw Driver

I learned the deepest lesson about chosen energy not in a boardroom, but from an auto-rickshaw driver in Delhi.

It was a sweltering afternoon. I was frustrated, running late for a meeting after a series of rejections. I jumped into an auto, my body tense, my mind already writing a script for failure.

The driver, a man in his fifties, turned to me with the most genuine, crinkly-eyed smile. "Kahan jaana hai, sahab?" he asked, his voice cheerful.

As we navigated the chaotic traffic, I noticed his auto was spotless. A small, fresh marigold was tucked near the meter. He hummed an old Bollywood tune, gracefully maneuvering through impossible gaps without a hint of anger.

I couldn't understand his positivity. "Bhaiya," I finally asked, "the traffic, the heat, the difficult passengers... how do you stay so positive?"

He chuckled. "Sahab, the traffic is not in my hands. The heat is not in my hands. But my attitude towards my word? That is my *maalik* (my boss). If I let the outside world decide my inside weather, I will have a storm in my heart all day long. But if I choose to be peaceful, then my shift is peaceful. And you know what? People like a peaceful driver. They pay fairly, they don't argue, and some become regulars. This smile," he said, tapping his cheek, "is not a reaction. It is my tool."

In that moment, I saw it clearly. He wasn't just driving an auto; he was the CEO of his own energy. He understood that his chosen attitude was his greatest business asset. He wasn't waiting for the world to be perfect to be happy; he was bringing happiness to his imperfect world, and the world was rewarding him for it.

The Ripple Effect of Your Energy

People often ask me: "How can I be positive when I'm having a bad day?"

My answer: **You don't have to be positive. You just have to act positive for 30 minutes.**

Here's the secret: Energy is contagious. When you bring positive energy into a conversation, something magical happens:

- On the phone, people can hear your smile. Your voice becomes warmer, your tone more engaging.
- In person, your energy fills the room before you even speak.
- In both cases, you create a space where people want to be, rather than have to be.

I've had prospects tell me, "I don't know what it is about you, but I just feel good talking to you." That's not a sales technique. That's the power of chosen positivity.

The 30-Minute Transformation: A Sales Story

Think of your energy not as a feeling, but as a practical tool—the most powerful one on your utility belt. You don't need to wait to feel motivated to use a hammer; you just pick it up and start driving nails.

I learned to "act positive for 30 minutes" during a brutal sales slump. I had made 47 calls with zero appointments. My spirit was broken. For the 48th call, I decided to run an experiment. I felt defeated, but I would *act* as if I had just closed my biggest deal.

I stood up at my desk, put on a massive, ridiculous smile that felt completely fake, and dialed. My voice was artificially bright. "Good morning, Mr. Desai! This is Himanshu. I'm having a fantastic day and hope you are too!"

There was a pause on the other end. Then, Mr. Desai, who probably expected yet another tired, robotic sales voice, chuckled. "Well, someone's cheerful. What's making your day so good?"

That fake smile had created a genuine moment of human connection. We ended up speaking for 15 minutes. He didn't need my service, but he referred me to two leads who did. That one call, made with manufactured energy, broke my slump and led to two closed deals.

Here's why this works like science:

- **Scenario A (The Default):** You've had a bad morning. You call a prospect with a flat, tired voice. The prospect, already busy, hears your lack of energy and feels justified in ending the call quickly. Their "I'm busy" is a reaction to your subconsciously communicated "This isn't important."

- **Scenario B (The Intentional):** You've had a bad morning. You take 10 seconds to reset your posture and smile. You call the same prospect with engaged, warm energy. They hear confidence and value. Even if they're busy, they're more likely to say, "Send me an email," or "Try me next week," because your energy has signaled that what you offer is worthwhile.

Your "acted" positivity isn't deception. It's a strategic decision to lead with your best self, especially when you don't feel like it. It tells the prospect, "I respect you and this opportunity enough to bring my A-game, regardless of my personal circumstances." That respect is contagious and builds trust faster than any claim you can make about your product.

The Noble Truth About Sales

Let me tell you why sales is the most noble profession in the world which is the reason you should be highly excited about it:

When you make a sale, you're not just earning a commission. You're:

- Solving someone's problem
- Helping a company grow
- Creating jobs for families
- Fueling the economy that supports us all

Every time I close a deal, I think about the ripple effect. That sale means someone can pay their employees. Those employees can feed their children. Those children can go to school. We are the engine that makes the business world move forward.

When you understand this, rejection stops being personal. It's not about you. It's about timing, fit, or circumstances.

This understanding gives you the resilience to hear "no" 99 times while still bringing your best energy to the 100th call.

Building Your Energy Muscle

This isn't about positive thinking. It's about positive practice. Here's how to build your energy muscle:

Morning Alignment (5 minutes)

Before checking emails, ask: "What problem will I solve for someone today? How will I make someone's life better?" This sets your intention for value creation, not commission chasing.

Pre-Call priming (30 seconds)

Before each call, stand up. Smile—even if you have to force it. Say out loud: "I'm about to help someone." Your biology follows your behavior.

Rejection Processing (60 seconds)

When you hear "no," don't internalize it. Say: "Thank you for your time. I wish you the best." Then physically shake it off—stand up, stretch, reset. Your next prospect deserves your best energy, not your last rejection.

Becoming the Person Who Sells

Early in my career, I thought sales was about mastering scripts and techniques. I would practice my lines, rehearse my responses to objections, and try to sound confident. This "acting" was an important first step - it gave me structure when I had none, and it was far better than approaching calls with fear.

But I noticed something about the truly great salespeople I admired. They weren't just good actors following scripts. There was something different about them - a genuine warmth, an authentic confidence that couldn't be faked. People weren't just buying from them; people enjoyed buying from them.

That's when I understood: **The goal isn't to act like a positive salesperson - it's to become one.**

Here's the transformation that changes everything:

When you only act positive:

- You exhaust yourself maintaining the facade
- Your energy feels forced, not natural
- The moment you face rejection, the act crumbles

When you become positive:

- Your energy becomes authentic and contagious
- You genuinely enjoy serving others
- Rejection doesn't break you - it fuels your growth

I learned to stop asking "How should I act?" and start asking "Who do I need to become?"

I needed to become the person who:

- Genuinely believes in the value they provide
- Sees every "no" as stepping stone to the right "yes"
- Understands that their positive energy might be the brightest part of someone's day
- Finds real joy in helping others succeed

This shift changed everything. Instead of forcing positivity, I started feeling it. Instead of rehearsing scripts, I focused on having genuine conversations. The techniques that once felt awkward became natural expressions of who I was becoming.

People don't just buy your product - they buy your energy. And they can tell the difference between someone who's acting positive and someone who genuinely is positive.

The Long Game

Sales isn't about today's commission check. It's about the person you become through thousands of conversations, countless rejections, and daily choices to show up with positive energy.

The prospects who said "no" to me years ago? Many of them became clients later. Why? Because they remembered the positive, professional energy I brought to our conversation. They remembered the salesperson who took rejection gracefully and kept moving forward.

Your energy today builds your reputation for tomorrow.

Your Turn:

Tomorrow, before your first call, I want you to do one thing: Stand up, smile like you just closed your biggest deal, and bring that energy to the conversation. Don't wait for the right mood. Create it.

The world doesn't need more salespeople following scripts. It needs more salespeople who understand that their greatest tool isn't their pitch—it's their presence. And that's a superpower anyone can develop.

CHAPTER 5

Mastering the Art of Questions

*You can have everything in life you want, if you will just help enough other people get what they want. – **Zig Ziglar***

Control the Conversation, Close the Deal:

Ask yourself-

When you're trying to convince someone for anything, what do you spend most of your time doing? Talking or listening?

If you're like I was in the beginning, you're probably talking. A lot.

You're explaining features, listing benefits, defending your price—performing a monologue hoping it hits the mark.

I used to think sales was about having the best arguments. I was wrong.

Sales is not about having the right answers. It's about asking the right questions.

The moment I learned this, I stopped being a pitchman and started becoming a partner. My deals didn't just grow; they became easier to close.

The 5 Deadly Sins of Sales Communication

Before we learn what to do, let's be clear about what *not* to do. I've been guilty of every one of these. They are the reason most salespeople struggle.

1. You Lose Control of the Call.

Here's a hard truth: in every sales conversation, someone will be sold in the end. It will either be you selling your product, or the prospect selling you on an excuse why they can't buy. **The person who controls the communication controls the sale.** If you're not guiding the conversation with questions, you are being guided by the prospect's objections.

2. You Don't Ask Questions.

This is the root of the problem. The moment you go into "answering mode," you lose your authority. You become a walking, talking brochure. And it's impossible to charge a premium when you're just an order-taker. **The one who asks the questions controls the communication, the relationship, and the outcome.**

3. You Don't Ask the *Right* Questions.

Your prospect isn't there to become your friend. They aren't bored. They are there because they have a serious problem and they are looking for a solution. Asking superficial questions like "Are you happy with your current provider?" kicks you out of the sale. You need questions that dig into the real pain.

4. You Talk Too Much.

This is a sin, especially in closing. Talking too much does three terrible things:

- It keeps you from discovering their real problems.
- It makes you look naive and amateurish.
- It gives the prospect more reasons to say no.
  People do not want to buy from an amateur, especially for high-ticket products. Silence is your friend. Let them fill it.

5. You Fail to Build Trust.

People buy people first, the product second. Most salespeople fail to build trust because of their own inner baggage: fear, limiting beliefs, desperation, and a need to seem perfect. This comes out in your communication. You talk too fast, you over-justify your value, you use cheesy old tricks. **People want to buy, but they hate to be sold to.** Trust is built when you stop trying to *please* them and start focusing on *understanding* them.

The Tale of the Questioning Salesman

Ramesh (name changed), an insurance agent from Bangalore, was polite, eager, and terrified of rejection. He spent his days explaining every detail to prospects, hoping they would buy. Weeks went by—his numbers barely moved.

One day, his VP asked: *"Are you solving their problem, or just talking about yourself?"*

Ramesh changed his approach. With a little help, he started asking questions like:

- "What worries you most about your retirement plan?"
- "If you don't invest now, how will it affect your family's future?"
- "Have you thought about how your children would manage if something unexpected happens?"

Something magical happened. His meetings transformed. He started discovering fears and desires his prospects hadn't even shared with their spouses. He wasn't convincing anymore; he was guiding. He was helping them see their own future more clearly.

His closure rate doubled in three months.

The lesson? **Questions are power.** Talking tells them you have a solution. Asking shows them they need one.

Why We Ask Questions: The 3 Reasons

Every question you ask should have a purpose. We don't ask questions just to make conversation. We ask them for three strategic reasons:

Discovery: To gather information. What is their situation? What is their problem? What have they tried?

Control: To gently guide the conversation. To steer it away from price and towards value, away from objections and towards solutions. The person asking the questions is the one in control.

Motivation: To make the prospect *feel* their need. A problem is just a fact. But when you ask, "How is this problem affecting you?" you help them connect to the *pain*. And pain is a powerful motivator to buy.

Our job is to use questions to convert a passive information-seeker into an active, motivated client who is ready to find a solution.

Why We Fear Asking Questions (And How to Stop)

I know what you might be thinking. "But, Himanshu, what if I ask the wrong thing? What if I offend them? What if I lose the deal?"

I get it. I've been there. That fear is real. But here's the hard truth I learned: that fear only exists when your pipeline is empty.

When you're desperate for *this one deal* to close, you can't afford to ask the real questions. You're too scared to rock the boat.

But when you've been consistently prospecting—when your calendar is full by following the White Space Principle—everything changes. You're not desperate. You're curious. You can ask the tough questions because you're not afraid of losing *one* client. You're focused on helping the *right* client.

A full pipeline gives you the courage to be a consultant, not a beggar.

The Story of Asking the Right Questions

Siddharth was struggling to sell a high-priced software solution to the owner of a mid-sized manufacturing unit, Mr. Agarwal. For two meetings, he had delivered what he thought was a perfect pitch. He explained every feature, every ROI calculation, every benefit. Mr. Agarwal listened politely, asked a few questions, and said he'd think about it. The deal was stalled.

Before the third meeting, Siddharth threw the script away. I advised him not to pitch and to only ask questions.

He walked in and said, "Mr. Agarwal, thank you for your time. I realize I've been talking a lot about my solution. Today, I'm here to listen. Can you help me understand what a perfect outcome looks like for you?"

Mr. Agarwal was slightly taken aback. "What do you mean?"

The Goal Question: "If you could wave a magic wand and fix one thing in your production process, what would it be?"

He thought for a moment. "The delays," Mr. Agarwal said. "There are always delays between the shop floor and the inventory room. We lose track."

The Problem Question: "What's causing those delays right now?"

"Manual data entry," he sighed. "The floor manager writes it down, it goes to the clerk, who types it into a system. Sometimes the handwriting is bad, sometimes the clerk is busy. Mistakes happen. Parts are lost."

The Impact Question: "When a part is lost or delayed, what is the real cost? How does that ripple through your business?"

His demeanor changed. This was no longer an abstract conversation. "The real cost?" he said, leaning forward. "Last month, we had to air-freight a critical component from Pune to Delhi to meet a deadline for a major client. It cost us ₹80,000. But the bigger cost was the panic, the overtime for the assembly team, and the fear of losing that client's trust. My production manager almost quit from the stress."

Mr. Agarwal had just handed Siddharth the value of his solution. No further explanation needed.

The Vision Question: "So, if you had a system that eliminated those delays and mistakes, giving you real-time data, what would that be worth? What would you be able to do with that peace of mind and the ₹80,000 you wouldn't be spending on emergency freight?"

He looked out the window, then back at Siddarth. "It would be priceless. I could finally sleep at night. I could focus on growing the business instead of fixing daily fires."

There was a long silence.

Finally, Mr. Agarwal spoke. "That software of yours... the one you showed me last time. Does it do that? Does it give real-time data from the shop floor?"

"It does," Siddharth said.

"Send me the agreement," Client said.

The salesperson had not mentioned the product once. He had not defended its price or explained a single feature. By asking questions, he guided the customer to uncover his own pain so acutely that the product became the obvious, necessary solution. The salesperson didn't close the sale. Client did.

Your Simple Framework for Any Conversation

You don't need to memorize 100 questions. Remember this simple flow. Your only job is to listen to the answers and ask the next logical "What" or "How" question.

1. **The Goal Question:** "What are you hoping to achieve with [a solution like] ours?" (Understand the ideal outcome.)
2. **The Problem Question:** "What's stopping you from achieving that right now?" (Uncover the current challenge.)
3. **The Impact Question:** "How is that problem affecting your [business, team, peace of mind]?" (Find the real pain and motivation.)
4. **The Vision Question:** "If we could solve that, what would that be worth to you?" or "What would that better situation allow you to do?" (Make them visualize the payoff.)

Stop Assuming, Start Asking

We all make up stories in our heads when we're scared.

- "He's too busy to talk."
- "She only cares about price."
- "They're happy with their current provider."

These stories are poison. They are based on our own fears, not their reality.

Your assumption is the mother of all missed opportunities.

In sales, assumptions are a silent killer. They cause you to pre-reject yourself, water down your pitch before you even deliver it, and walk away from deals that were there for the taking. When you assume, you are fighting a phantom opponent of your own creation instead of learning the real rules of the game.

The professional cost of assumption is staggering. You might assume a prospect is all about price, so you lead with discounts and train them to devalue your service. You might assume they're loyal to a competitor, so you never uncover the deep-seated frustrations they're secretly hoping to solve. You are leaving money on the table and letting your own fears negotiate against you.

Don't fall into this trap. You must replace assumption with curiosity. Your primary job is not to talk, but to uncover. The real sale, the one that builds unshakeable trust and commands premium prices, is never in the first answer they give you. It's hidden beneath the surface, in the emotional and financial impact of their problem.

Your most powerful tool to find it isn't your pitch—it's a question.

The Final Shift: From Seller to Guide

When you master the art of asking, the game changes; you stop selling and start helping. Your prospect is no longer being pitched to; they are being understood.

They arrive at the solution themselves, with you as their guide.

So, before your next meeting, don't just prepare what you're going to tell them.

Prepare what you're going to ask them.

Your turn:

Think of one client you'll speak to this week. Write down the list of questions that will ask them (not the interrogation)

Go on, be curious.

CHAPTER 6

Building Unshakable Trust

*"Trust is the glue of life. It's the most essential ingredient in effective communication. It's the foundational principle that holds all relationships". — **Stephen Covey***

The Psychology of Sales:

Let me ask you a question that haunted me for years.

Why is it that two salespeople can say the exact same words, yet one gets a "I'll think about it" and the other gets a signed contract?

For the longest time, I thought it was about the pitch. I spent nights polishing my scripts, believing the perfect sequence of words was the magic key.

I was wrong. Dead wrong.

The key wasn't in the script; it was in the space *between* the words. It was in the silent language of trust. The real sale happens not when you're talking, but in the quiet moments when your prospect is deciding if you are a person of your word.

Story of Vikram and Ajay: A Lesson in Perceived Authority

A Meerut based SAAS company had a sales team of about twenty salespeople. But when a tough problem arose, everyone turned to one of two men: Vikram or Ajay.

Vikram was the charismatic talker. He could charm anyone. He knew all the latest industry gossip and was the life of the party. But when a client asked a deeply technical question or a contract needed complex negotiation, Vikram's charm would falter. He'd talk faster, deflect, or make a vague promise. People liked him, but they didn't bring him their biggest, most fearsome clients.

Then there was **Ajay**.

Ajay was calm, almost quiet. He never rushed to speak. When you asked him a question, he would pause, consider it, and then answer with a depth that showed he wasn't just reciting a manual—he truly understood the *why* behind everything.

Everyone once saw him handle an angry client who was ready to cancel a six-figure deal. Vikram had tried to sweet-talk him and failed. Ajay walked in, sat down, and said, "I've read the case. That sounds incredibly frustrating. Tell me, from your perspective, where did we go wrong?"

Then he did something extraordinary. He stayed silent for a full thirty seconds while the client vented. He didn't interrupt, justify, or explain. He just listened.

When the client finished, Ajay didn't apologize immediately. He said, "You're right. Our implementation team failed to meet the standard we promise. Here is my plan to fix it, personally." He laid out a clear, concise plan.

The client not only stayed—he upgraded his contract six months later.

Ot was clearly the psychology of trust in action. Ajay wasn't just selling a product; he was projecting an **aura of unshakable competence and integrity.** He was the expert, not because he said so, but because everything about him—his silence, his listening, his decisive action—proved it.

"The most important thing in communication is hearing what isn't said." — Peter Drucker

Ajay heard what wasn't being said: the client needed to be heard and needed a leader to take control. I decided then: I would learn the psychology behind becoming an Ajay.

The Psychology of Trust: The Invisible Sale

Here's a truth that changed my career:

People don't buy from the best salesperson; they buy from the salesperson who makes them feel safest.

That's what trust really is — **emotional safety**.

When your prospect feels they can rely on your words, your expertise, and your integrity, price becomes secondary.

And you can *engineer* that feeling.

Let's break down the psychology behind trust into **five pillars**.

1. The Principle of Authority — Be the Expert Everyone Respects

Humans are wired to trust authority.

We look up to pilots, doctors, lawyers — people who *know their stuff*.

In sales, authority doesn't mean bragging. It means **quiet competence** — the kind Ajay projected.

How to demonstrate authority:

- **Know more than your competitor.**
  Read your industry news. Study your client's ecosystem. Be aware of trends before they are.
- **Teach before you pitch.**
  If in every meeting you teach your prospect one new thing about their own process, you become their *go-to advisor*, not a vendor.
- **Answer with data and depth.**
  Never wing it. "I think" sounds uncertain. "Here's what the numbers show across the industry" sounds credible.
- **Respect your competition.**
  When you bad-mouth a rival, you reveal insecurity. A professional says:
  "They're strong in X. We've chosen to focus on Y because it helps clients achieve Z."
  Confidence without arrogance breeds trust.

2. The Principle of Likability — Win the Human Before the Deal

You've heard it: *People buy from people they like.*
But "likable" doesn't mean cracking jokes or being overly friendly. It means **authentic alignment** — showing that you *see* and *understand* the person in front of you.

How to build genuine likability:

- **Mirror, don't mimic.**
  Match your client's pace and tone naturally. Fast talker? Keep up. Thoughtful and slow? Mirror that calm energy. It creates subconscious harmony.

- **Find real common ground.**
  It could be as small as "I also love working early mornings — it's quiet time to think."
  Real, human similarities create micro-bonds of trust.
- **Be vulnerably confident.**
  Don't fake perfection. "That's a good question — we actually struggled with that in our early phase, but here's what we learned..."
  Authenticity beats artificial polish.

"People don't care how much you know until they know how much you care." — Theodore Roosevelt

3. The Principle of Congruence — When Words and Energy Match

The fastest way to lose trust? Say one thing and *signal* another. Your tone, eye contact, and posture — they all broadcast truth or doubt.

Trust signals through body language:

- **The Power of the Pause:** Ask a question and *stay quiet.* The one who speaks first loses psychological control.
- **Speak slowly.** Fast speech screams anxiety. Calm speech radiates certainty.
- **Stillness equals strength.** The best closers move less when talking. Every gesture is purposeful, never fidgety.
- **Eye contact without aggression.** You're not staring down — you're staying anchored.

Watch TED speakers. The best ones don't rush because they *own the room.*

You must own your meetings the same way.

4. The Principle of Value First — Be the Consultant, Not the Closer

A desperate seller cannot be trusted. The moment you *need* the deal, you lose power.

The paradox of sales is this:

When you detach from the outcome, you gain control of it.

Instead of "How do I close this sale?", think: "Can I genuinely solve this problem?"

If the answer is no — have the integrity to say so.

That act alone earns permanent respect.

Ask questions like:

- "What would success look like for you six months from now?"
- "Is this problem costing you more in time or in money?"
- "Based on what we discussed, does this feel like the right fit for you?"

When you sound like a *partner* instead of a *pitchman*, the buying resistance melts away.

5. The Principle of Consistency — Keep Micro-Promises

Most salespeople think trust is built in big moments — it's not. It's built in the *micro moments* — showing up on time, following up when you said you would, sending that promised document the same day.

Every fulfilled promise is a micro-deposit in your "trust account." Every missed one is a withdrawal.

If you ever wonder why a deal feels cold despite a great pitch, check your consistency.

The Story of the Defence Battery and the Unlikely Partner

For two years, my company had tried to sell a high-precision machinery unit to a manufacturer who supplied critical batteries for defence contracts in India and Israel. The client, a fiercely patriotic ex-army man named Colonel Sinha, had a simple, unshakeable rule: **"My production line for national security projects cannot stop. Not for an hour."**

Every salesperson before me had hit the same wall. We offered the best machine with the best warranty. But Colonel Sinha saw only one thing: risk. "What happens if it breaks down? What if my operator makes a mistake? I cannot have a delay. The answer is no."

I realized I wasn't selling a machine; I was being asked to sell a guarantee against operational risk—a guarantee no piece of machinery alone could ever provide.

So, I stopped selling the machine.

I went back to Colonel Sinha and said, "Sir, I understand. The machine is not the solution. The solution is a system that makes failure impossible. Give me one week."

For the next seven days, I didn't act like a salesman. I became a project manager. I leveraged my network and found a reputable service company that could provide certified, on-call technicians. I then connected with another client of ours, a non-competing manufacturer, and negotiated a standby agreement where they could supply a limited number of the critical parts in an absolute emergency.

I returned to Colonel Sinha not with a brochure, but with a **battle plan**.

"Sir," I presented. "Here is the proposal. You get the machine. But you also get this: a dedicated, trained operator from our service partner for the first month, at our cost. A 6-hour service guarantee, 24/7, for any issue. And a backup supply chain for your most critical components, so your line never halts. We are not just selling you equipment; we are embedding ourselves as a part of your operational integrity."

I had taken his biggest fear—downtime—and built a fortress of solutions around it. The machinery became just one component in a much larger, risk-free package.

Colonel Sinha reviewed the plan. He looked up, and for the first time, he smiled. "You didn't try to sell me a machine. You sold me peace of mind. You have my order."

The deal that had been dead for two years was closed in two days.

The Trust Lesson: When you stop selling your product and start architecting solutions for your client's deepest fears, you transcend the vendor relationship. You become a strategic partner. You don't just provide a tool; you become the bedrock of their confidence. That is the highest form of trust in sales.

The Story of the Printer That Couldn't Print Trust

My friend, Jatin, was trying to win over a family-run packaging business in Delhi. The owner, Mr. Gupta, was a tough, no-nonsense man in his sixties who had built his company from scratch. Jatin's predecessor had failed to sell to him for years, warning, "He doesn't trust anyone, especially not salespeople."

Jatin's first meeting was a disaster. He came in with his best pitch, his polished presentation on his tablet, and all the data. Mr. Gupta listened for five minutes before holding up a hand.

"Beta," he said, pointing to an old, ink-stained printer in the corner of his office. "That printer is older than you. Every salesman for ten years has told me to replace it. They show me speed, cost-per-page, wireless features. Do you know why it's still here?"

Jatin didn't.

"Because it has never once failed me during a critical job. Not once. Your fancy promises mean nothing. This machine's reliability means everything."

Jatin had been selling the wrong thing. He was trying to sell a new printer. Mr. Gupta was buying **trust**.

Jatin left, humbled. A week later, he went again without his laptop. He didn't mention the printer. Instead, he asked one question: "Mr. Gupta, what does a 'critical job' look like for you?"

He sighed, but he answered. It led to a conversation about a missed delivery deadline the previous year that had cost him a major client. He spoke about the anxiety of equipment failing when his reputation was on the line. He wasn't worried about print speed; he was terrified of **betrayal**.

Jatin finally understood. He wasn't there to sell a machine. He was there to prove he could be as reliable as that old printer.

Our company didn't just sell printers; we provided a guaranteed 4-hour, 24/7 on-site service. Instead of leading with the printer's specs, Jatin secured a meeting for him with our Head of Service Operations. He didn't ask for the sale. He gave Mr. Gupta a direct phone number and said, "This is Rohan. If any machine we install ever causes a delay, you call him. He is your guarantee."

Mr. Gupta didn't buy a printer that day. He bought a **promise**, backed by a person and a plan. He bought the certainty that he would never lose a client to equipment failure again.

The lesson was clear: **Trust isn't built on features; it's built on proof that you understand and will safeguard what your client values most.** For Mr. Gupta, that was his reputation for reliability. Jatin had to become a part of his insurance policy, not just another salesman with empty promises.

The Three Levels of Trust

As I've seen over years in the field, all client relationships evolve through three levels:

1. **Credibility Trust:** "Can this person actually deliver?"
   Built through product knowledge, case studies, data.
2. **Reliability Trust:** "Will this person do what they say?"
   Built through consistency, responsiveness, and accountability.
3. **Emotional Trust:** "Does this person truly have my best interest at heart?"
   Built through empathy, listening, and genuine care.

Every sale that lasts years travels through all three.

The Final Word: You Are the Product

The best way to find out if you can trust somebody is to trust them.
— *Ernest Hemingway*

Before a client invests in your solution, they are investing in you. They are buying the confidence you radiate, the understanding you demonstrate, and the security you guarantee.

The stories in this chapter show a clear evolution:

- **Ajay** built trust through **Credibility**.
- **Jatin** built trust through **Connection** and **Reliability**.
- **I** was able to built trust through **Partnership**.

This is the architecture of unshakeable trust. It moves from "Can this person do the job?" to "Is this person on my team?"

Trust is not a tactic; it is your identity as a sales professional. It is the currency that allows you to command premium prices, weather any negotiation, and build a reputation that attracts clients to you.

Stop focusing on being the best talker in the room. Start focusing on being the most trustworthy person in your industry.

Your turn:

This week, in your next client interaction, your only goal is to practice **The Pause and The Principle of Authority.** After they ask a question, pause for three full seconds before answering. Then, answer not just with a feature, but with a piece of expert insight—teach them something.

Feel the shift. You are no longer a seller. You are the source. And that is a position of unshakable power.

CHAPTER 7

The Myth of "I Can't Afford It"

"Price is what you pay. Value is what you get." — ***Warren Buffett***

How to Charge Premium:

Why does a person who hesitates to spend ₹50 on a cup of coffee, willingly pay ₹300 for the same coffee at a fancy cafe?

Why does a man who negotiates ruthlessly over ₹10 on vegetables, walk away and light a cigarette that costs him ₹20?

For years, I thought my products were too expensive. I'd hear "It's too costly" and my heart would sink. I'd immediately think about discounting, or worse, I'd believe them. I thought I was failing because I was pricing people out.

I was looking at it all wrong.

The problem was never the price. The problem was my inability to build a bridge between my price and their perception of value.

The problem is never the money in their wallet. It's the value in their mind.

The Universal Law of Premium

Look around you. Premium isn't an exception; it's a rule in every single industry.

- **Airlines:** You have economy, business, and first class. Everyone arrives at the same time, but some pay 5x more for a better experience.
- **Coffee:** You can get a caffeine fix for ₹50 or a "experience" for ₹300.
- **Barbers:** A haircut can cost ₹100 or ₹1000. You're not just paying for hair on the floor; you're paying for the chair, the ambiance, the skill, and the feeling of being taken care of.

If you are not charging a premium, it does not mean people will not pay a premium. It just means they won't pay *you* a premium. They are happily paying it to someone else who has convinced them of the greater value.

The Story of the ₹500 Belt

I remember trying to sell a high-quality leather belt for ₹500. The shopkeeper pointed to a similar-looking one on his rack. "This one sells for ₹200. Yours is too expensive."

I went home that day defeated. I thought, "He's right. My belt is too costly."

A few weeks later, I was in a different part of the city and saw a man in a showroom selling a belt for ₹2,500. And people were buying it!

I stood there and watched. He wasn't just handing over a belt. He was telling a story. He talked about the Italian leather, the artisan who crafted the buckle, the way it would age and develop a unique character. He wasn't selling a belt; he was selling an identity—a piece of sophistication.

The ₹200 belt held up pants. The ₹2,500 belt elevated a man's entire self-image.

That's when I realized: **People don't buy products; they buy better versions of themselves.**

The Trap of Charging Low

Early on, I thought the key was to be the cheapest. It was a race to the bottom, and I was always losing.

Here's the brutal truth about competing on price: **If price is your only weapon, you must be the absolute lowest. Second place gets you nothing.**

But being the cheapest is a dangerous game.

- **Low Margins:** You have no buffer. One slow month can wipe you out. You can't invest in better materials, marketing, or your own growth.
- **No After-Sales Support:** How can you provide excellent customer service, replacements, or support when you're barely making a profit? You can't. This leads to unhappy customers and a damaged reputation.
- **The Worst Customers:** The customers you attract with low prices are the most demanding. They will squeeze every ounce of your time for the rupee they've paid. They are loyal only to the price, not to you. The moment someone cheaper comes along, they are gone.

Now, contrast this with a premium customer.

- They have chosen you for your value, not your discount.
- They complain less because their expectations are aligned with the premium experience.
- They often become your biggest advocates, *justifying your cost to themselves and others*. They say things like, "It's worth it for

the peace of mind," or "The quality is just different." They sell for you.

The Story of Manoj and the ₹50,000 Projector

Manoj, was struggling to sell high-end projectors to schools. His product was ₹50,000. The standard alternative was ₹20,000. For months, he heard the same refrain from every principal: "Your price is more than double. It's just not in the budget."

Manoj kept pitching the superior specs: higher lumens, better resolution, longer lamp life. He was selling features, and he was losing.

Then he met Principal Iyer of a prestigious private school. Before he could start his presentation, she held up a hand. "I know your projector is good, Manoj. But why should I spend my entire annual technology budget on it when I can buy two others for the same price?"

Manoj closed his brochure. He knew he had to change his entire approach.

"Madam," he said, "let's forget the projector for a moment. What is the single biggest challenge your teachers face in the classroom?"

She didn't hesitate. "Student engagement. Especially the children in the back. If they can't see the board clearly, they lose focus. Their grades slip, and then we have to deal with concerned parents."

There it was. The real pain.

Manoj continued, "And when a projector bulb fails in the middle of a lesson, what is the impact?"

"At least 20 minutes of learning is lost," she sighed. "The disruption derails the entire class. It's a teacher's nightmare."

Now, Manoj could architect the value. He wasn't selling a projector; he was selling a solution to her most critical operational and reputational pains.

"Madam," he explained, "my projector isn't just brighter. Its clarity ensures every child, even in the last row, can see the finest details on a diagram, which directly addresses that engagement challenge. But more crucially, it has an instant-on feature and a bulb life of 10,000 hours. That's five years without a single disruption. No more wasted 20-minute segments. How much is 20 minutes of productive learning time, every day, for five years, worth to this school?"

He had masterfully shifted the conversation from the **cost of his product** (₹50,000) to the **cost of her problem** (disrupted classes, disengaged students, unhappy parents).

Principal Iyer was silent, mentally calculating the true value. The ₹30,000 price difference was no longer an expense; it was a strategic investment in educational consistency and student success.

She bought the projector that day. Not because it had more lumens, but because Manoj had built a bridge of value that connected his price directly to her deepest frustrations. He solved for the pain, and the product became the obvious answer.

The Lesson: The price is never the real obstacle. The failure is in not connecting that price to the client's cost of inaction. When you make the pain of the problem feel more expensive than your solution, the sale becomes inevitable.

People Afford What They Want to Afford

I used to see people buying homes on 20-year EMIs, cars on 5-year loans, and the latest iPhone on monthly installments.

Someone would say, "They can't afford it."

But they *were* affording it. They were rearranging their entire financial lives for it. Why?

Because the **emotional value** of that house—the security, the status, the pride—was higher than the financial cost. The joy and social signal of that new car or iPhone was more valuable than the money.

Money is never the problem; it is the perceived value.

When the perceived value of your solution exceeds the price tag, the offer becomes a no-brainer. The question shifts from "Can I afford it?" to "Can I afford to *not* have it?"

The Reasons People Buy for

So, how do you build this perceived value? You must understand the two fundamental engines that drive every human decision. People pay money for one of two reasons:

1. **To Escape Pain:** This is the stronger motivator. The desire to avoid loss, fear, frustration, or embarrassment is far more powerful than the desire for gain.
    - *Examples:* Buying insurance to escape the fear of poverty. Buying a new CRM to escape the pain of a chaotic, unproductive team.
2. **To Achieve a Goal:** The desire for gain, status, improvement, or a dream.
    - *Examples:* Buying a premium course to achieve a promotion. Buying a luxury car to achieve a feeling of success.

Your job is no longer to sell a product. Your job is to be a doctor of desire.

You must diagnose whether your prospect is running *away* from something (pain) or *towards* something (a goal). Then, you must show them, with absolute clarity, that your product is the fastest, most reliable vehicle to get them there.

The Final Word: Become a Value Architect

Once I understood that "I can't afford it" was just a smoke screen for "I don't see enough value," everything changed.

I stopped being a beggar and became an architect. I stopped defending my price and started constructing value, brick by brick, until my offer stood as a majestic skyscraper next to the crumbling shack of their problem.

Your price is not the barrier. Your inability to build a compelling vision of the solution is.

"He who can no longer pause to wonder and stand rapt in awe, is as good as dead; his eyes are closed." — Albert Einstein

Make them pause. Make them wonder. Make them stand in awe of the future you can build for them. When you do that, the price becomes a minor detail on the blueprint of their new life.

Your turn:

Think about your product or service. Answer this: If your prospect says, "It's too expensive," what *pain* have you failed to magnify, or what *goal* have you failed to make desirable?

CHAPTER 8

The Three Levels of Pain

*"Your prospect's 'why' is your most powerful 'how'." — **Himanshu Mittal***

How to Uncover the Real Cost:

Your prospect will only tell you the surface-level problem. The real sale is buried underneath.

I learned this the hard way. A client once told me, "We need a new 3D Printer"

I took him at his word. I spent an hour showing him how amazing my machinery was. I gave him specs, benchmarks, the works.

He thanked me and said he'd think about it. He bought similar machinery from a competitor.

When I got the courage to ask why, I realized "My 3D machine was good. But the other salesperson made him realize that the slow speed of his printer was causing his team to waste 20+ hours a week on product development. They were frustrated and quitting. He didn't sell the customer a fast 3D Printer; he sold them a way to stop their team from falling apart."

However I was selling the same product but I had been solving the wrong problem. I was treating a symptom, not the disease.

I was stuck at the surface. To bring real change, you have to be willing to dig for the deep, emotional root. You have to uncover the **Three Levels of Pain.**

The Anatomy of a Problem: The Three Levels

Think of yourself as a doctor. A patient comes in and says, "My head hurts." (Surface Pain). A bad doctor would just prescribe a painkiller. A good doctor asks, "How did it happen? Is it a throbbing pain? How is this affecting your work and sleep? What are you unable to do because of it?"

You must be a good doctor.

Level 1: Surface Pain – The "What"

This is the symptom. It's the stated, logical reason they're talking to you. It's the tip of the iceberg.

- *Example (Real Estate):* "We need a 3BHK apartment."
- *Example (Insurance):* "My current policy is expiring."
- *It sounds like:* A simple, factual statement of a need.

Level 2: Business Pain – The "So What"

This is the consequence of the Surface Pain. It connects the problem to their wallet, their efficiency, or their responsibilities.

- *Your Question:* "I understand you need a 3BHK. What's the main challenge with your current home?" / "If your policy were to lapse, what would the immediate financial impact be?"
- *The Answer (The Pain):* "Our current 2BHK is too small, my wife and I are both working from home now, and it's impossible to focus." / "We'd have no safety net if the primary earner had a medical emergency."

- *It sounds like:* "It's costing us money/time." / "It's making us inefficient."

Level 3: Personal Pain – The "Now What"

This is the gold. This is the emotional core—the fear, frustration, anxiety, or desire that keeps them up at night. This is the *real* cost you can solve.

- *Your Question (The Master Key):* **"How does that situation make you *feel*?"** or **"What is the real cost of that for you and your family, beyond the money?"**
- *The Answer (The Gold):* "It's putting a strain on our marriage. We're constantly snapping at each other and the kids because there's no space to breathe. I feel like I'm failing to provide a proper home." / "I lie awake worrying that if I get sick, my children's education will stop. The thought of not being able to protect them is terrifying."

Most people get stuck at Level 1. That's why they compete on price. They're all selling the same band-aid for the same scratch.

When you uncover the **Level 3: Personal Pain**, you are no longer selling a commodity. You are selling a specific, emotional solution. You are selling peace of mind, pride, security, or freedom. And for that, there is no price tag. **People will pay a premium to end a deep, personal pain.**

The Framework in Action: From Symptom to Cure

Let's see how this works in a real scenario: **Selling a High-End Air Purifier.**

- **You:** "What made you start looking at air purifiers?" *(Goal Question)*

- **Client:** "The pollution in Delhi is just unbearable these days." **(Surface Pain - The 'What')**
- **You:** "I understand completely. How is the poor air quality affecting your day-to-day life at home?" *(Problem Question - digging for Business Pain)*
- **Client:** "We can't even keep the windows open. My son has started developing a constant cough and allergies, and we're spending a fortune on doctor's visits and medication." **(Business Pain - The 'So What' - it's costing health and money)**
- **You (digging for Personal Pain):** "That sounds incredibly stressful. As a parent, what's the hardest part about seeing your son struggle with this?"
- **Client (The emotional core is revealed):** "The hardest part? It's the guilt. I feel like I'm failing as a parent because I can't even give him clean air to breathe in his own home. Every time he coughs, it feels like my fault. I just want him to be healthy and safe." **(Personal Pain - The 'Now What')**

Boom.

You just moved from "bad pollution" (a general problem) to "my failure as a parent and my child's health is at risk" (a profound, personal pain).

Now, when you present your air purifier, you're not selling a machine with a HEPA filter. You're selling "a solution to a mother's guilt," "a guarantee of her child's health," and "the peace of mind that her home is a true sanctuary." The ₹40,000 price tag is no longer a cost; it's an investment in her child's well-being and her own emotional relief.

Become the Master of the Problem, Not the Solution

Most salespeople rush to master their solution. They memorize every feature, every technical spec, and every benefit. They become walking, talking brochures.

This is a fatal mistake.

You cannot prescribe a cure if you haven't diagnosed the disease. A doctor who immediately recommends surgery without asking about your symptoms isn't a genius—they're a danger.

Your prospect doesn't care about your solution. They care about their problem. The more deeply you understand their problem—its roots, its impact, its true cost—the more indispensable you become.

Crafting the "No-Brainer" Offer

Once you know the Level 3 Pain, your final job is to craft an offer that is impossible to refuse. A "no-brainer" isn't about being the cheapest; it's about making the value so overwhelming that the decision is automatic.

People will pay anything to come out of their pain. Your offer is the bridge.

Here's how to build that bridge:

1. **Anchor the Real Cost:** Remind them of the pain's price.
    - *"You mentioned the constant doctor's visits are costing you ₹5,000 a month, not to mention the emotional toll..."*
2. **Present Your Solution as the Cure:** Frame your product as the direct antidote to their specific pain.
    - *"This air purifier is your guarantee of a safe, healthy home for your son. Imagine the relief of seeing him play without coughing, and the money you'll save on medical bills."*

3. **Overcome the Final Hurdle with Irresistible Value:** Make the transition risk-free and easy.
    - **The Risk Reversal:** "And to make this an absolute no-brainer, it comes with a **10-year warranty**. If it ever stops working, we replace it. No questions asked."
    - **The Bonuses:** "When you decide today, I'll also include **two years of free filter replacements** (a ₹12,000 value), so you have zero maintenance costs."
    - **The Scarcity/Urgency:** "I only have five units at this guaranteed price this month due to high demand."

The "No-Brainer" Formula:
(Anchor their Pain) + (Your Solution as the Cure) + (Risk Reversal + Bonuses) = An Offer They Can't Refuse

Your offer isn't a cost; it's a smaller, fixed investment that eliminates a larger, escalating pain. The brain doesn't need to deliberate. The path is clear.

Real-World Genius: How Apple Sells the Problem First

Look at one of the most successful marketing campaigns of all time: Apple's "Get a Mac."

They didn't start by listing the Mac's processor speed or RAM. They started by mastering—and dramatizing—the PC's problems.

A typical ad showed a young, casual guy (the Mac) next to a slightly frumpy, older man (the PC). The PC would freeze up, crash, get viruses, and struggle with simple tasks. He was constantly frustrated, slow, and unreliable.

Apple wasn't selling a computer. They were selling an escape from the daily frustration and humiliation of using a clunky PC.

They made you feel the problem first: the wasted time, the lost work, the sheer annoyance. By the time they presented the Mac, it wasn't just a product—it was a hero, the obvious solution to a pain they had just made you relive.

They sold the problem so well that the solution sold itself.

Your product is just a tool. Your prospect's problem is the masterpiece.

Study the masterpiece. Understand every brushstroke of their frustration, every color of their fear, the entire canvas of their operational chaos.

When you can articulate their problem better than they can, when you can connect it to a real financial or emotional cost, you stop being a salesperson. You become a diagnostician. And the diagnosis always points to your solution.

The Final Word: Sell the Cure, Not the Pill

Armed with the true, emotional cost of their problem, you are no longer a salesman discussing price. You are a doctor prescribing a cure.

When you solve a Level 3 pain, you are not a cost. You are an investment. You are the solution to what hurts them most.

Stop selling the features of your pill. Start selling the freedom from their pain.

Your turn:

Think of your most common customer. Write down the typical answers for all three levels for them:

1. **Surface Pain:** What do they initially say they want? (e.g., "a 3BHK")
2. **Business Pain:** What is the practical consequence? (e.g., "no space to work, inefficient")

3. **Personal Pain:** What is the underlying fear, frustration, or desire? (e.g., "I feel like a failure who can't provide for my family.")

This three-layer map is your most powerful tool to justify your premium and close deals that feel less like transactions and more like transformations.

CHAPTER 9

The Objection is a Ghost

"The obstacle in the path becomes the path. Never forget, within every obstacle is an opportunity to improve our condition." — ***Ryan Holiday***

Unmasking the Real Barrier:

What's the first thing you feel when a prospect says, "Let me think about it," or "It's too expensive"?

If you're like I was, your heart sinks. Your stomach tightens. You see the deal—the commission, the recognition, the relief—slipping through your fingers. You start to panic.

For years, I saw objections as a wall. A solid, immovable "NO" that I had to somehow break down with my words.

I was wrong.

An objection is not a wall. It's a curtain. And behind that curtain isn't a "no"—it's a question they don't know how to ask.

But before we can pull back their curtain, we must first face our own.

The Real Objection Lives in Your Mind

The fear of hearing "no" is more powerful than the "no" itself. This fear comes from one place, and one place only: a thin pipeline.

When you are desperate for *this one deal* to close, every objection feels like a life-or-death threat. Your energy becomes needy. Your voice carries a hint of panic. The prospect can smell your fear, and it makes them trust you less.

Remember the White Space Principle from Chapter 3? This is where it becomes your psychological armor.

When your calendar is full, an objection is just feedback. When your calendar is empty, an objection is a rejection.

A full pipeline gives you the power of detachment. You can listen calmly, diagnose the real issue, and help them—because you're not afraid of losing them. You are a doctor, not a beggar. The prospect feels this shift in energy, and it makes them more open, not more defensive.

The first person you need to handle is yourself.

The Apartment That Wasn't About the Color Scheme

An up-and-coming interior designer, Priya, landed a meeting with a wealthy, young couple who had just bought a new apartment. They loved her portfolio and her vision for their space. After an enthusiastic two-hour consultation, the wife smiled awkwardly and said, "We love your ideas, Priya. We just need to think about it. Your fee is a bit higher than we anticipated."

Priya's heart sank. Her old instinct was to immediately justify her hours or offer a small discount. But she remembered the principle: isolate the objection.

She leaned forward calmly and said, "I completely understand. Investing in your home is a big decision. Let me ask you a hypothetical: If my fee were exactly within your budget, would you be ready to hire me and get started on this vision next week?"

The couple exchanged a look. The husband shifted in his seat. "Well... to be perfectly honest, probably not," he said. "We're just a bit overwhelmed. This is our first premium home. We're worried that... well, what if we don't like the final result? What if it looks great in your drawings but feels wrong when it's all built? We'd be stuck with it."

Boom. The ghost was unmasked.

The objection was never the designer's fee. It was the fear of making a costly, permanent mistake. "It's too expensive" was a smokescreen for "We're terrified of regret."

Priya didn't lower her price. Instead, she addressed the real objection. "That is the most important concern you could have," she said. "And it's exactly why my process is structured the way it is. Before we hammer a single nail, we do a 3D virtual walkthrough. You'll 'live' in the digital version of your home. You can change the paint, move the furniture, and see the sunlight at different times of day. You will be 100% confident before we begin. My fee isn't just for a design; it's for your peace of mind."

She then showed them a portfolio of client testimonials that specifically mentioned this worry and how the process alleviated it.

The couple signed the contract at her full fee that afternoon. The real sale wasn't on interior design; it was on confidence and risk-elimination.

Smoke in the Mirror: The Art of Isolating the Objection

Most objections are not real. They are smokescreens. They are the easiest thing for the prospect to say, not the real thing stopping them.

They say: **"It's too expensive."**

What they often mean: *"I don't see enough value yet,"* or *"I have another concern I'm not telling you."*

Your job is not to defend your price. Your job is to find out what's *really* going on. You do this with one powerful technique: **Isolating the Objection.**

The goal is to discover if the stated objection is the *only* thing stopping them.

The Isolation Question:

"I understand. Let me ask you a hypothetical question: **If we could solve [the price/timing/feature concern], is this the solution you would move forward with right now?"**

Watch their reaction closely.

- **If they say, "YES, absolutely!"**
  Then you have successfully isolated the objection. Now you can have a productive conversation about value. The deal is still alive.
- **If they hesitate and say, "Well, no, actually..."**
  Then you've just discovered the smoke. You have now politely called their bluff and can address the real issue.
    - *You respond:* "I see. So [the price] isn't the main thing. What would you say is the *biggest* thing holding you back?"

This simple question separates the truth from the excuse.

The Solar Solution and the Stubborn Factory Owner

Ajay was a determined solar energy consultant trying to sell a rooftop solar system to Mr. Gupta, the owner of a mid-sized textile factory in Surat. Mr. Gupta had initially been interested, acknowledging the rising electricity costs from the grid. But as they reached the proposal stage, he shut down.

"Too expensive, Ajay," Mr. Gupta said, waving a hand dismissively. "The capital investment is too high. The payback period is too long. I can't justify it."

Ajay, like any good salesperson, had tried to handle this. He presented detailed ROI calculations, showed government subsidy schemes, and even offered a tie-up with a financing partner for easy EMIs.

Mr. Gupta's response was a classic Indian market objection: "*Sahi hai, par abhi nahi.* It's good, but not right now. Let's revisit next financial year."

The deal was stuck. Ajay knew the numbers were solid. He knew Mr. Gupta stood to save lakhs of rupees. But the objection of "price" was a wall he couldn't break through.

He decided to change his approach. He requested one final meeting, not to present, but to understand.

"Mr. Gupta," Ajay began, "I respect your position on the investment completely. You've seen the numbers. Can I ask just one question, off the record?"

Mr. Gupta nodded cautiously.

"If the price was not an issue at all—if this system was free—would you install it tomorrow?"

Mr. Gupta leaned back in his chair, a faint smile on his face. "Well, of course. Who wouldn't want free electricity?"

"That's my point, sir," Ajay said softly. "So the *concept* isn't the problem. The value is clear. That tells me my job isn't to convince you about solar; it's to solve the hurdle of the upfront cost. But I feel there's something else. Is it *just* the price, or is there another reason now isn't the right time?"

He used the classic isolation technique: *"Is it just the price?"*

The room was silent for a moment. Mr. Gupta sighed, the defensiveness leaving his posture.

"Between us, Ajay?" he said, his voice lower. "It's not just the price. My eldest son is starting his own export business next month. All my liquid capital is going there. It's his dream. I can't tell him 'no' to fund a solar system, even if it saves me money. The *izzat* of my son, his future... that comes first. The risk is not the solar system; the risk is diverting funds from my son's launch."

There it was.

The real objection wasn't "price." It was **priorities and paternal duty.** The "smoke" of a financial objection cleared to reveal the "mirror" of a father's love and commitment.

Ajay didn't push the EMI option again. Instead, he said, "Mr. Gupta, that is a fantastic reason. And a father's support for his son's dream is the most important investment of all. What if we could structure this in a way that requires zero capital from you *this year*? We have a new partner-led model where they own the system and sell you the power at a fixed, lower rate than the grid. You start saving from day one with no upfront cost. Your son gets his funding, and you still cut your operating expenses. We protect your capital and your son's future at the same time."

Two weeks later, Ajay closed the deal. Not by fighting the price objection, but by discovering the real pain underneath: a father's desire to support his son without compromising his business's efficiency. He solved for the *real* problem, and the "price" objection melted away.

The Framework: Handle the Objection, Don't Fight It

Once you've isolated the real objection, follow this simple framework. Your mindset is not to "win," but to "understand and solve."

Step 1: Pause and Validate (Don't Pounce)

When you hear an objection, your first job is to shut up and listen. Then, validate their concern. This builds trust.

- *What to say:* "That's a fair question." or "I appreciate you bringing that up."

Step 2: Isolate the True Objection

Use the magic question to see if it's the real barrier.

- *What to say:* "Just so I understand correctly, if we could solve the [price/timing/feature] concern, is there anything else that would stop you from moving forward?"

Step 3: Answer with a Question (Uncover the Root)

Before you launch into your defense, ask a question to understand the *why* behind their objection.

- *For "Price":* "I understand it's an investment. What were you comparing this price to?" or "What would the solution need to be worth for the price to feel like a no-brainer?"
- *For "I need to think about it":* "Of course. What part of this would you like to think about most? Is it about the fit, the timing, or something else?"

Step 4: Revisit the Value (The Cure for their Pain)

Once you understand the root, bring the conversation back to the Level 3 Pain you uncovered and the value of the solution.

- *What to say:* "I understand the concern about the timeline. It makes me think back to what you said about your team's frustration. If we wait another quarter, what is the cost of that continued frustration for you?"

The Final Word: The Objection is the Path

An objection is not a stop sign. It is a signpost. It points you directly to what your prospect needs to feel safe, secure, and confident in their decision.

Your fear of it is your own ghost. Slay it with a full pipeline.

Their stated objection is often a ghost. Unmask it with a single, courageous question.

When you stop fearing objections and start welcoming them as clues, you stop being a salesperson and start being a problem-solver. And problem-solvers don't get rejected; they get hired.

Your turn:

Think of the most common objection you hear. Now, write down your "Isolation Question" for it.

Your script:

1. Pause & Validate: "I understand..."
2. Isolate: "Just to be sure, if we could solve [that objection], would you be ready to move forward?"
3. Uncover the Root: "What's the main reason behind that?"

Practice this. The next time you hear an objection, smile. The ghost has appeared, and you know exactly how to make it vanish.

CHAPTER 10

The Digital Lever

"Visibility isn't vanity—it's survival. In the digital age, the salesperson who refuses to show up online is invisible to the very clients searching for answers."—***Unknown***

Your Profile is Your New Storefront:

Why Digital Matters More Than Ever?

When you entered sales, you probably imagined knocking on doors, making calls, attending events, and chasing leads through crowded streets. For generations, that's how the game was played. But today, the real opportunities are invisible—and that invisibility could be costing you every single day.

While you're making calls, others are closing deals while sipping chai in their living rooms. Your next big client is scrolling, searching, networking online. If you aren't visible there, you simply don't exist.

Pain Point: The cost of staying offline or ignoring LinkedIn isn't just lost leads—it's lost credibility, lost trust, and lost revenue. In a world where buyers do their homework before responding to your pitch, your digital reputation is often your only chance to make a first impression.

My Story: Losing Deals to Ghosts

Early in my career, I relied solely on phone calls and in-person meetings. I hustled from sunrise to sunset, burning through energy just to get 30 decision-makers on the phone. But then, something strange happened: deals began slipping through my fingers. Prospects were polite but distant, often saying, "We've already spoken to another expert online." My pitch was solid. But I was invisible.

One day, frustrated, I ran a simple experiment. I Googled myself and found... nothing. No website, no LinkedIn, no proof I was credible or trustworthy. It was a wake-up call: sales isn't just about working hard, it's about being seen where opportunity lives.

The LinkedIn Wake-Up

LinkedIn is not an online resume—it's the largest virtual marketplace for your deals, relationships, and reputation. Over 180 million senior decision-makers and 10 million C-suite executives log in every week. Every day you spend invisible here, your competition gets ahead.

- Your Profile: It's your new storefront. A buyer who lands on your profile must instantly feel "This person helps people like me solve problems I care about."
- Your Posts: These are your silent sales pitches. Each post is an evergreen flyer that establishes you as an expert, even when you're asleep.
- Your Network: Your real power isn't just in the number of connections, but in the value and engagement you generate for the right audience.

Action Steps: Your Digital Playbook

1. Build the Foundation: The Profile Overhaul

- Headline: Replace your job title ("Insurance Agent") with a promise-based headline ("Helping Mumbai's families secure wealth & peace of mind").
- Photo & Banner: Use a crisp, friendly photo and a cover image that resonates with your market.
- About Section: Don't write a bio, write a short story—who you help, how you help, why it matters.
  Example: "I grew up in a house where every rupee mattered. Today, I help other families build financial security with insurance solutions designed for the realities of Indian life."

2. Content That Converts: Become a Value Machine

- Post 2–3 Times a Week:
  Share real stories ("My client invested in this policy and avoided X challenge"), FAQs ("Why is term insurance critical?"), or mistakes to avoid.
- Educational Videos: Break down complicated topics into 1–2 minute videos. A simple explainer on "How much insurance is enough?" can drive huge engagement.
- Celebration Posts: Highlight client wins, but make them about the client, not yourself. ("Congrats to Rahul for buying his first home!").
- Ask for Engagement: End each post with a question ("What's the #1 money worry in your family?") or a call to connect for free advice.

3. Grow Authority through Community

- Join Niche Groups:
  For real estate, insurance, or any sector, join both professional and consumer groups ("Moms in Mumbai", "Startup India").
- Help First:
  Answer questions, troubleshoot problems, share tips. If someone asks about "safe investment options for NRI families," reply with a checklist.
- Share Research:
  Post links to interesting reports or case studies, always adding your own insights ("Here's what this means for small business owners in India").

4. Outreach Scripts That Work

- Connection Message Example:
  "Hi [Name], noticed your recent milestone at [Company]. Congrats! I specialize in helping professionals like you safeguard their wealth as they advance. If you ever want to exchange insights, happy to connect."
- Follow-up Message:
  "Hi [Name], saw your question in [Group] about [topic]. I've helped several clients with similar challenges. Let me know if you'd like tailored advice—no pitch, just experience."

5. Trigger-Based Networking

- Alerts for Milestones:
  Set reminders for when a contact changes jobs, celebrates a

business anniversary, or posts about a new life event. Use these to message with genuine congratulations and offer value.
- Digital Listening:
Track what your prospects like, comment on, and share. Respond thoughtfully—don't just pitch, start conversations.

The Hidden Power: Relationship, Not Reach

A viral post means nothing if your DMs are empty. The real goal is private conversations leading to booked calls and genuine trust.

- Treat outreach as a gentle knock—never a sales pitch.
- Avoid generic offers; tailor your script ("I see you lead a team—what's the #1 challenge your team faces with digital prospecting?").
- Use voice notes occasionally; a warm tone builds instant connection.

Templates & Exercises
LinkedIn Post Formula

1. Problem: "Many business owners lose money because they don't understand the risk in their current insurance."
2. Personal Story: "I learned this the hard way when my client's family faced X."
3. Solution: "A simple step—comprehensive term insurance—turned everything around."
4. Call to Action: "Tag someone who needs this advice or DM me for a free checklist."

Profile Checklist

- Headline: Promise-driven, specific
- Banner: On brand, relevant
- About: Story > Resume
- Experience: Results-oriented, with numbers
- Recommendations: 2–3 real testimonials
- Skills: Relevant, endorsed

Your Turn (End-of-Chapter Tasks)

1. Audit your LinkedIn profile today for clarity, authenticity, and value.
2. Draft three stories from recent client wins and schedule them as weekly posts.
3. Pick two LinkedIn groups and answer five questions—focus on providing solutions, not pitching products.
4. Note five milestones in your network (job changes, birthdays, anniversaries) and send personalized messages congratulating or supporting.
5. Track one week of inbound leads/comments and reflect on which content sparks the most engagement.

Advanced Digital Moves: The Power of Automation

- Use tools like LinkedIn Sales Navigator for targeted lead lists.
- Employ simple automations for reminders, event tracking, and follow-up messages, but personalize every interaction.
- Test post timing and format (polls, images, PDFs) for maximum local market engagement.

Stories from the Field

Rohan's LinkedIn Revival

Rohan, a Pune-based real estate agent, once struggled with cold calls and low response rates. After rebranding his LinkedIn profile and posting simple videos explaining local property trends, he noticed a surge in inbound inquiries. Within 60 days, he closed two deals that came from LinkedIn posts—not a single cold call required.

Meena's Insurance Authority

Meena, early in her insurance career, struggled with price objections and trust. She began sharing client testimonials, case studies, and tips for budgeting insurance on her LinkedIn feed. Not only did her authority in local groups skyrocket, but she started receiving DM referrals from strangers congratulating her on her transparent advice. Digital trust translated directly into sales.

The Mindset: From Seller to Community Builder

You are more than a salesperson. In the digital world, you're a guide, a coach, and a storyteller. Every online interaction contributes to your brand.

- Don't chase vanity metrics—chase impact.
- Share your learning journey, mistakes, and wins openly; vulnerability inspires trust.
- Position yourself as the problem-solver for your niche, not just another "seller."

Final Thoughts: The Digital Salesman's Creed

Every time you post, comment, or engage online, remember you're planting seeds. Some will sprout instantly. Others will nurture roots that lead to future deals, partnerships, and lifelong clients.

You have a unique story, a solution, and a mission. If you want to thrive in today's sales battlefield, become the digital expert your competition is still struggling to understand.

Update your profile. Share your story. Give more than you sell. The next big client is online, searching tonight—will they find you, or someone else?

Ready for your next step? Take action—and watch offline hustle meet digital mastery.

CHAPTER 11

Epilogue — From Scarcity to Significance

"The boy who had nothing now has everything — but not the way he imagined."

If I could go back in time and find that 19-year-old boy—the one sleeping on a hungry stomach, with two shirts to his name and the taste of railway dust on his tongue—what would I say?

I wouldn't show him a bank statement. I wouldn't show him the keys to a nice car or a photo of a sleek office.

I would simply sit beside him, put a hand on his shoulder, and let him cry. I would let him pour out all the fear, the shame, the crushing weight of being a burden. And when he was done, I would look him in the eye and tell him the one thing he needed to hear:

"You are enough. Just as you are. And this pain is not the end of your story; it is the foundation of your strength."

The journey you have read in these pages was never just about sales. It was never just about money. It was a journey from **scarcity to significance.**

The Emptiness of the Full Bank Account

I achieved what I once dreamed of. I made money. I could afford a home, good food, and security for my family. The ghost of poverty that haunted my childhood was finally silenced.

But a strange thing happened when I reached that summit. I looked around and felt a quiet emptiness. The hunger that had driven me—the raw, desperate need to escape—was gone. And in its place was a question: **"Is this all there is?"**

I realized I had been climbing the wrong mountain. I was so focused on escaping the valley of scarcity that I didn't stop to ask what was on the peak. Money was a threshold, not a destination. It got me through the door, but it couldn't tell me how to live in the house.

The real transformation began when I shifted my focus from what I could *get* to what I could *give.*

The Real Win: Meaning Over Money

The most profound success of my life is not a deal I closed or a bonus I earned.

It is the message from a young salesperson who read my story and said, "If you can do it, so can I."

It is the ability to look a struggling client in the eye and say, "I understand your fear, and I know the way out," because I have lived it.

It is the quiet dignity of being able to provide, not just for myself, but for others who stood where I once stood.

This is **significance.** It's the impact that outlives you. It's the wealth you create in the hearts and minds of others. Money buys comfort, but meaning buys fulfillment.

The frameworks in this book—the inner game, the art of the question, the psychology of trust—are not just sales tactics. They are the tools I used to rebuild myself. They are the principles that taught me how to connect, how to serve, and in doing so, how to finally heal the invisible boy who just wanted to be seen.

I'd love to hear from you about how this book has impacted your sales journey. Feel free to send me a message at https://www.linkedin.com/in/himanshu10x/.

I may not respond immediately but I read every message and will get back as soon as I can. Your success matters to me.

A Final Word to You

You picked up this book to learn how to sell. I hope I have taught you that. But if you take only one thing from my story, let it be this:

Your past does not define your value. Your present circumstances do not dictate your future. Your greatest sale will always be the one you make to yourself—the decision to believe in your own significance long before the world sees it.

The journey from scarcity to significance is not a straight line. It's a spiral. You will circle back to your old fears, but each time, you will be stronger, armed with the lessons from your falls and the confidence of your climbs.

Sell well. Build a great life. But most importantly, build a meaningful one.

The world isn't waiting for another successful salesperson. It's waiting for **you**—the one who has been forged in struggle and now operates with wisdom, empathy, and purpose.

Your story is not over. It is just beginning.

Himanshu Mittal

9 789355 924957

Printed at Repro India Ltd.